CW00419184

THE FUNNIEST RUGBY QUOTES... EVER!

Also available

The Funniest Tennis Quotes... Ever!

The Funniest Football Quotes... Ever!

The Funniest Cricket Quotes... Ever!

The Funniest Chelsea Quotes... Ever!

The Funniest West Ham Quotes... Ever!

The Funniest Spurs Quotes... Ever!

The Funniest Arsenal Quotes... Ever!

The Funniest Man City Quotes... Ever!

The Funniest Newcastle Quotes... Ever!

The Funniest United Quotes... Ever!

The Funniest Leeds Quotes... Ever!

The Funniest Boro Quotes... Ever!

The Funniest Forest Quotes... Ever!

The Funniest Sunderland Quotes... Ever!

The Funniest Leicester Quotes... Ever!

The Funniest Saints Quotes... Ever!

The Funniest Everton Quotes... Ever!

The Funniest Villa Quotes... Ever!

The Funniest Celtic Quotes... Ever!

The Funniest Rangers Quotes... Ever!

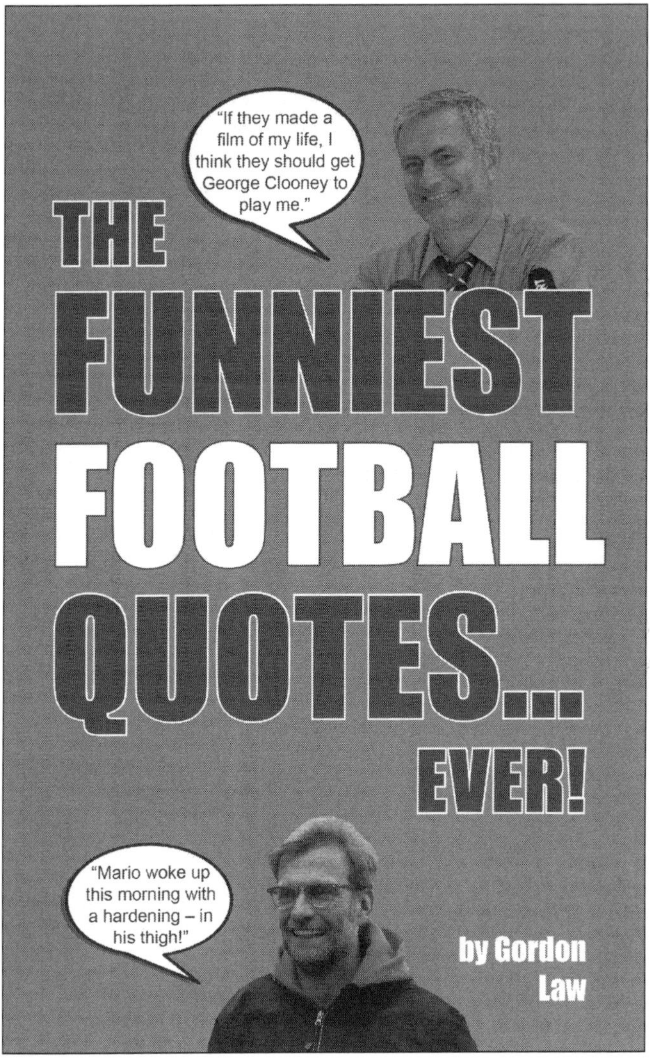
"If they made a film of my life, I think they should get George Clooney to play me."
THE FUNNIEST FOOTBALL QUOTES... EVER!
"Mario woke up this morning with a hardening – in his thigh!"
by Gordon Law

Printed in Europe

ISBN: 9798863998558
Imprint: Independently published

Photos courtesy of: Shutterstock.com/mountainpix; Shutterstock.com/atsportphoto

Contents

THE FUNNIEST RUGBY QUOTES... EVER!

GAME FOR A LAUGH

"You can knock seven bells of sh*t out of each other and have a pint with him afterwards."

Welshman Adam Jones on rugby

"In 1823, William Webb Ellis first picked up the ball in his arms and ran with it. And for the next 156 years forwards have been trying to work out why."

Sir Tasker Watkins, president of the Welsh Rugby Union

"Playing in the second row doesn't require a lot of intelligence really."

England captain Bill Beaumont

"I'm pleased to say I don't think about rugby all the time... just most of the time."
England legend Lawrence Dallaglio

"Rugby backs can be identified because they generally have clean jerseys and identifiable partings in their hair... come the revolution the backs will be the first to be lined up against the wall and shot for living parasitically off the work of others."
Australia's Peter FitzSimons

"A forward's usefulness to his side varies as to the square of his distance from the ball."
Wellington boss Clarrie Gibbons

Q: "What's the difference between the professional 2001 Lions and the 1989 squad?"

Donal Lenihan: "We've been together three-and-a-half days and we haven't been to the pub yet."

"Referees are only human, I think."

Australia's Phil Kearns

"Rugby is just like love. You have to give before you can take. And when you give the ball it's like making love – you must think of the other's pleasure before your own."

France full-back Serge Blanco

"You've got to get your first tackle in early, even if it's late."

Wales centre Ray Gravell

"Once you're on the pitch, it's chaos. I find it faintly amusing, this view that some people have of the captain, clicking his fingers and saying, 'Guys, let's try plan B' and everyone goes, 'Oh God, yes, plan B'. That's b*llocks."

England star Will Carling

"The backs preen themselves and the forwards drink."

England No.8 Dean Richards

"They have this impression of English rugby that we all play in Wellington boots and we play in grass that is two foot long."

England coach Sir Clive Woodward

"The main difference between playing league and union is that now I get my hangovers on Monday instead of Sunday."

Tom David of Wales

"Rugby players are either piano shifters or piano movers. Fortunately, I am one of those who can play a tune."

A modest Pierre Danos

"If you can't take a punch, you should play tennis."

French coach Pierre Berbizier

"Nobody in rugby should be called a genius. A genius is a guy like Norman Einstein."

New Zealand's Jono Gibbes

"I don't know why prop forwards play rugby."

England scrum half Lionel Weston

"Get your retaliation in first."

Welsh second row Carwyn Jones

"You cheat and cheat until you get caught out and then you cheat some more, you've really got to play on that edge."

Wales' Brent Cockbain

"If the game is run properly as a professional game, you do not need 57 old farts running rugby."

Will Carling

"Sure there have been injuries and deaths in rugby – but none of them serious."

All Blacks' team doctor John 'Doc' Mayhew

"If you're a ref and you want the big appointments, you've got to lick the backsides of some of the top nations."

Namibia head coach Dave Waterston

"You have 15 players in a team. Seven hate your guts and the other eight are making their minds up."

Coach Jack Rowell

"It's basically the same, just darker."

New Zealand's Kevin Senio on how evening games compare to the day

"You need a mental toughness and probably don't need to be too bright."

Mark Regan on playing in the front row

"I don't think you can win this World Cup without scoring points."

Aussie coach John Connolly

"I'd rather hit the ball than be the ball."

South Africa's Hennie le Roux prefers golf to coaching rugby

"Beer and rugby are more or less synonymous."

All Blacks' Chris Laidlaw

"Forwards are the gnarled and scarred creatures who have a propensity for running into and bleeding all over each other."
Peter FitzSimons

"League is much, much more physical than union, and that's before anyone starts breaking the rules."
Wales' Adrian Hadley

"Abuse directed at the ref is self-explanatory – or kept simple enough so he'll at least understand it."
Justin Brown

"It's bloody horrendous in League One, all graft and no fun."

Australian Drew Hickey

"As you run around Battersea Park in them, looking like a cross between a member of the SAS and Blake's Seven, there is always the lingering fear of arrest."

Brian Moore on England's new rubber training suit

"What makes rugby so special is that there is always room for the smaller man."

Irishman Conor O'Shea

"If you're being poked in the eye or punched...
you act accordingly. Some back off, some go
for blood."
Wales' Scott Gibbs

"I think you enjoy the game more if you don't
know the rules. Anyway, you're on the same
wavelength as the referees."
Jonathan Davies

"It's the first time I've been cold for seven
years. I was never cold playing rugby league."
**Wales star Jonathan Davies on his return to
rugby union**

SAY THAT AGAIN?

"If history repeats itself, I should think we can expect the same thing again."
New Zealand's Anton Oliver

"Losing to New South Wales is like masturbating, or losing a golf ball. You feel really remorseful afterwards but you know it will happen again if you're not careful."
Australia's Chris 'Buddha' Handy

"To play the game you have to play on the edge, but unfortunately he's gone to the edge of the cliff and jumped off it."
British Lions head coach Warren Gatland on Dylan Hartley's suspension

"Sometimes you are unlucky. Sometimes you get what you deserve. And sometimes you get a kick in the nuts."

Northampton's Christian Day

"The way to get out of the poo is to fight with people who are prepared to get in the trenches with you."

London Irish coach Brian Smith

"You never want to be that guy who talks it up and then can't back it up, training like Tarzan and playing like Jane."

England's James Haskell

"If you go out to get revenge on a team, you'll get bit on the a*se."

Ireland's Sean O'Brien

"We're showing signs of getting better. It's a pity the tournament is over now."

Scotland's Kenny Logan

"There's no such thing as a lack of confidence. You either have it or you don't."

England's Rob Andrew

"We are committing our own suicide."

Scotland coach Ian McGeechan

"A good defender should be so mean that if he owned the Atlantic... he still wouldn't give you a wave."

South Africa captain Morne du Plessis

"Sometimes you have to put your balls on the line."

British Lions head coach Warren Gatland on dropping Brian O'Driscoll

"Yes, it's a very humbling part of the game. You can dominate one day and get your pants pulled down on another."

Australia coach Michael Cheika

Q: "What's it like to play alongside Martin Johnson with the Lions?"

Brian O'Driscoll: "Knowledge is knowing that a tomato is a fruit; wisdom is knowing not to put it in a fruit salad."

"We have self-belief in each other."

Scotland great Gavin Hastings

"I will handle things the Brian Clough way. Whenever a player has a problem we will talk about it for 20 minutes and I will listen carefully to what he has to say. Then we'll agree that I was right."

Head coach Sir Clive Woodward

Say That Again?

"Let me use an analogy. I have a Staffordshire bull-terrier. Every time I feed it osso buco, he eats it like it's his last meal. And I think I'm like, and the team's like, my Staffordshire bull terrier. When it comes to meal times, that's how hungry, how passionate we are."

Australia legend George Gregan

"Scotland may have to go to some dark places, but we'll bring some torches."

Scots' coach Scott Johnson

"The first half will be even. The second half will be even harder."

Wales' Terry Holmes

"I had breakfast with my wife for the first time in a long time. At least I still think she's my wife, I don't know if she still thinks I'm her husband."

Japan coach Eddie Jones after their World Cup elimination

"You guys pair up in groups of three, then line up in a circle."

Hurricanes head coach Colin Cooper

"Ultimately you get what you deserve and we deserved what we got."

Northampton's Paul Grayson

"Youngsters need heroes. They need figures like Batman, Tarzan and Naas Botha."
Abie Malan of South Africa

"Last year we were all sizzle and steak, this year we had a horror start but now we are off like a bride's nightie."
Australia's Nick Cummins

"All we're doing effectively is chasing a pig's bladder around a field, but we still have the ability to touch so many people."
England's Josh Lewsey

RUCKING HELL

"The French are predictably unpredictable."

Andrew Mehrtens after a shock All-Blacks defeat

"You blindfold yourself and spin around for 10 times and then open your eyes and try to chase it down."

Canada coach Ric Suggitt prepares for Fiji's attacking style

"The only thing you're ever likely to catch on the end of an English back line is chilblains."

Australia's David Campese

"We are not calling them the All Blacks this week. They are New Zealand. New Zealand is a poxy little island in the South Pacific."

Assistant Australia coach Scott Johnson

"We play a similar style of rugby to England but we have better-looking players."

South Africa hooker Schalk Brits

"Wales have always had it in them to play this kind of no-fear, high-velocity rugby. But it's not an easy trick to pull off if you haven't got the ball."

England's Martin Johnson

"Wales is not an easy country to coach because, basically, the Welsh are lazy."

Former Scotland coach Jim Telfer

"The French pulled up the Scots' kilts and discovered they had no balls."

New Zealander Zinzan Brooke

"For the first time ever, we are all cheering for England tonight."

Johnny Sexton on 6 Nations Super Saturday as Ireland needed England to beat France to win the Championship

"Look what these b*stards have done to Wales. They've taken our coal, our water, our steel. They buy our houses and they only live in them for a fortnight every 12 months. What have they given us? Absolutely nothing. We've been exploited, raped, controlled and punished by the English – and that's who you are playing this afternoon."

Phil Bennett's pre-match team talk

"We've lost seven of our last eight matches. The only team that we've beaten was Western Samoa. Good job we didn't play the whole of Samoa."

Wales' Gareth Davies

"They were outstanding. They are the best team in the world by one minute."

Australia coach Eddie Jones on the 2003 England side

"The only memories I have of England and the English are unpleasant ones. They are so chauvinistic and arrogant."

Imanol Harinordoquy of France

"They can talk the talk, but they didn't walk the walk, did they?"

Richard Cockerill after England's 1999 win over Ireland

"It doesn't matter whether it's cricket, rugby union, rugby league – we all hate England."

Australian rugby union chief executive John O'Neill on their World Cup opponents

"Foul play and cheating are the two factors that can make the game unplayable... the All Blacks are guilty of both."

Wales star Clem Thomas

"I think the French always niggle, grabbing blokes around the balls and the eyes and that sort of thing."

Aussie coach Tim Lane

"Nobody ever beats Wales at rugby, they just score more points."

New Zealand's Graham Mourie

"The relationship between the Welsh and the English is based on trust and misunderstanding. They don't trust us and we don't trust them."

Ex-RFU secretary Dudley Wood

"Next weekend is going to be a tough one. Whatever happened against New Zealand. Australia are a different bag of hammers."

Ireland's Eddie O'Sullivan

"We are going to bash each other for 80 minutes and then enjoy a good chat and maybe a beer afterwards."

South Africa's Duane Vermeulen on New Zealand

"The All Blacks are a myth. We need to demystify all this. We're not going to the abattoir."

France coach Bernard Laporte ahead of their World Cup tie against New Zealand

"The Irish treat you like royalty before and after the game, and kick you to pieces during it."

England's Jeff Probyn

"My coaching reputation has probably gone up in smoke, but I really don't care. You want to cry for these guys. But at the end of the tournament I told them to go and get p*ssed and to be proud of themselves."

David Waterston after Namibia's 2003 World Cup exit

"If we have to play against New Zealand, I'll explain it like this. To win, their 15 players have to have diarrhoea and we will have to put snipers around the field shooting at them and then we have to play the best match of our lives."

Argentina's Juan Martin Fernandez Lobbe

"Of all the teams in the world you don't want to lose to, England's top of the list. If you beat them, it's because you cheat. If they beat you, it's because they've overcome your cheating."

New Zealand's Grant Fox

"As far as the English are concerned, I have decided to adopt the same attitude as them. I despise them as much as they despise everybody else. And as long as we beat England, I wouldn't mind if we lost every other game in the 6 Nations."

Imanol Harinordoquy

"I'm trying to think of the last bar room brawl I was in. Is it going to be like that? It's probably a fair assumption; I quite like that. A nice clean bar brawl, though, with none of the dirty stuff. No gouging or glass throwing. Just the clean stuff. It's going to be tasty. They are very, very aggressive at the breakdown. Ireland loves chucking numbers in there."

England's Joe Marler on the 6 Nations game against the Irish

"We're playing against a team that hate you and want to beat you up or beat you in the game."

Jack Nowell ahead of England's clash with Wales

"The French selectors never do anything by halves; for the first international of the season against Ireland they dropped half the three quarter line."

Nigel Starmer-Smith

"No leadership, no ideas. Not even enough imagination to thump someone in the line-up when the ref wasn't looking."

JPR Williams on Wales' defeat to Australia

"We French score tries because we cannot kick penalties."

Jean-Pierre Rives

TALKING
BALLS

"I would have liked nothing more than to knock him out."

South Africa's Corne Krige on Matt Dawson

"Will Carling epitomises England's lack of skills. He has speed and bulk but plays like a castrated bull."

David Campese

"I think we would struggle to get that one through."

Eddie Jones on a story that South Africa players are not allowed women or alcohol at the World Cup

"Colin has done a bit of mental arithmetic with a calculator."

Ma'a Nonu

"Fijian full-back Waisale Serevi thinks 'tackle' is something you take fishing with you."

Jonathan Davies

"Tony Ward was the most important rugby player in Ireland. His legs are far more important to his country than even those of Marlene Dietrich were to the film industry. A little hairier, maybe, but a pair of absolute winners."

Mike Gibson hails his countryman

"He was like Luke Skywalker in Star Wars, when he has his hand lopped off and keeps coming back again."

Jeremy Guscott on Jonny Wilkinson's England return

"I'm sure the lads will be glad to see him gone. There'll be more food for everyone else now!"

Austin Healey on Jason Leonard retiring

"Love me or hate me. I don't hate anyone. Peace and love. I just don't like Cocks."

Toulon's Martin Castrogiovanni does not miss coach Richard Cockerill at Leicester

"As long as my backside is pointing to the ground, Ewen McKenzie will not coach Australia."

Unnamed Australian rugby union official

"Brian, what are you going to do for a face when Saddam wants his a*se back?"

Peter Clohessy to Brian Moore during the England v Ireland clash

"Mike [Ford] may be a bit upset and that's fine. What did he say? That I missed my mum? Who doesn't miss their mum?"

Sam Burgess responds to the coach

"Dean Richards is nicknamed Warren, as in Warren ugly b*stard."

Jason Leonard of England

"I thought Hans Christian Andersen had come back from the dead."

RFU's Martyn Thomas on reports that Sir Clive Woodward was returning to England

"I think Brian Moore's gnashers are the kind you get from a DIY shop and hammer in yourself. He is the only player we have who looks like a French forward."

Paul Rendall on his teammate

"He's the sort of player whose brain doesn't always know where his legs are carrying him."
Nick Farr-Jones on David Campese

"I might give him a hug, as long as it doesn't get too awkward. We wouldn't really be huggers really; it's more of a high five or a handshake but we'll see what happens."
Paul O'Connell on his farewell to Brian O'Driscoll

"He's a guy who gets up at six o'clock in the morning regardless of what time it is."
Colin Cooper on New Zealand's Paul Tito

"He's the kind of player you expect to see emerging from a ruck with the remains of a jockstrap between his teeth."

Sir Anthony O'Reilly on Kiwi Colin Meads

"A figure who inspires hero worship among even those who think a fly half is a glass of beer."

Robert Philip on Jonah Lomu

"He is a very big boy -– I wouldn't like to be paying his food bills!"

USA coach Peter Thorburn on Henry Bloomfield

"He is banned from tweeting. The next time he does that I will break both his ankles."
Leicester chief Richard Cockerill after Jordan Crane revealed his injury on Twitter

"What will his legacy be? The semi-final victory over New Zealand was his best performance. But unfortunately, he will be remembered for the misguided rhetoric and unfulfilled promises."
Clive Woodward after Eddie Jones' sacking

"I told him, 'Son, what is it with you... ignorance or apathy?' He said... 'I don't know and I don't care'."
David Nucifora on fellow Kiwi Troy Flavell

"On the Lions tour in 1997, Mark Regan and Barry Williams blew up, but it was literally handbags."

Jeremy Guscott

"The sooner that little so-and-so goes to rugby league, the better it will be for us."

England's Dickie Jeeps on Gareth Edwards

"I've seen better centres in a box of Black Magic."

Joe McPartlin on his replacements in the Oxford University backs

"He's the biggest niggler of all time. That makes me laugh. The boy from Queanbeyan who niggles everyone, complaining about niggle. That's a bit like the pot calling the kettle black."

Eddie Jones after Australia's Nic White said England players were out for niggle

"Bloody typical, isn't it? The car's a write-off. The tanker's a write-off. But JPR comes out of it all in one piece."

Gareth Edwards after JPR Williams was involved in a road traffic accident

IN THE
SIN BIN

"It's better than being called a plonker."

Jason Leonard on being picked as one of the Lions' stars in a win over the All Blacks

"I want to reach for 150 or 200 points this season, whichever comes first."

New Zealand's David Holwell when asked about the upcoming season

"If they're going to call you this superhuman player or whatever and you believe it, then you should also believe it when they call you a t*sser."

Martin Johnson

"I may not have been very tall or very athletic, but the one thing I did have was the most effective backside in world rugby."

Ireland's Jim Glennon

"Me? As England's answer to Jonah Lomu? Joanna Lumley, more likely."

Damian Hopley

"It takes two hours to get ready – hot bath, shave my legs and face, moisturise, put fake tan on and do my hair – which takes a bit of time."

Wales' Gavin Henson

"I feel like I am the captain of the Titanic."

Dave Waterston after Namibia lose 142-0 to Australia

"Don't ask me about emotions in the Welsh dressing room. I'm someone who cries when he watches Little House on the Prairie."

Bob Norster

"It was the first time I've ever felt like a boy in a man's body. I was absolutely sh*tting myself."

Zinzan Brooke appearing for the All Blacks against South Africa in 1992

"It went well. There are no problems, and as a bonus, it showed that I have a brain!"

South Africa's Corne Krige after going for a brain scan

"Personally I wouldn't go there. You must get bored sh*tless in Newcastle."

Montpellier owner Louis Nicollin

"I can't really remember the names of the clubs that we went to."

All Black Chris Masoe when asked if he had visited the pyramids while in Egypt

"I had 52 messages on my phone within an hour of the final whistle and some were from people I'd never heard of, which was a bit worrying."

England coach Brian Ashton after victory over Australia

"I'm just off for a quiet pint; followed by 15 noisy ones."

Gareth Chilcott after his final game for Bath

"The time for reminiscing is after rugby. Then you can sit down and get fat."

Josh Lewsey

"I'm still an amateur, of course, but I became rugby's first millionaire five years ago."
David Campese

"In my time, I've had my knee out, broken my collarbone, had my nose smashed, a rib broken, lost a few teeth, and ricked my back. But as soon as I get a bit of bad luck I'm going to quit the game."
JW Robinson

"You still have egg and chips, Chinese from the same takeaway and your hair cut at the same place."
Will Greenwood after England's World Cup win

"Being dropped and Take That splitting up on the same day is enough to finish anyone off."

England's Martin Bayfield

"I've got a bottle of Johnnie Walker Blue. I'm going to consult it tonight and come up with a plan."

Namibia coach Dave Waterston prepares for Australia after losing to Argentina

"I don't know what the opposite of divisive is, but I'm the opposite of divisive."

Lawrence Dallaglio when asked what he thought about criticism directed at him

"I owe a lot to my parents, especially my mother and father."

New Zealand's Tana Umaga

"Maybe it would help if I was a foot taller, had hair and didn't look like a pit bull."

Richard Cockerill

"It's because of rugby I've got dodgy ears."

Phil Greening of England

"I've never had major knee surgery on any other part of my body."

New Zealand's Jerry Collins

"If I had been a winger, I might have been daydreaming and thinking about how to keep my kit clean for next week."

Bill Beaumont

"I'm going to graduate on time, no matter how long it takes."

All Black Rodney So'oialo on university

"Jeez, I've never met the president of a country before."

Irish star Malcolm O'Kelly was naked when Australia's prime minister John Howard entered the dressing room

"I've got to slink home now in disguise because I still live in Bath. We got a stuffing."

Richard Hill

"The knee doesn't trouble me when I'm walking. But it's painful when I kneel, like before my bank manager."

David Leslie of Scotland

"Basically I am like a dog – I just run after a ball."

England's Chris Ashton

"Salads don't win scrums."

Cake-loving South Africa prop Ox Nche

"I yell and scream like they do. I'm the worst of them. Totally. I'm a nightmare. Once they gave me the passport, that was it – I started throwing my hands in the air, drinking red wine and flying off the handle."

New Zealand coach John Kirwan on living in Italy

"All I ask is that when people object to my ways, is that they stab me in front not the back."

David Moffett on being appointed chief exec of the Welsh RFU

"It's only a thumb, I've got another one."

Wales captain Ryan Jones

Tadhg Furlong: "I never dreamed of captaining Ireland as a youngster."

Reporter: "What did you dream of?"

Furlong: "Spuds, gravy, the mother's Sunday roast."

"I know my talks can be a bit long-winded – but I didn't realise they were boring enough to send even my own brother to sleep."

Lions captain Gavin Hastings' team talk was too much for Scott

"The lads say my bum is the equivalent of one 'Erica'."

Bill Beaumont

MEDIA
CIRCUS

"I never comment on referees and I'm not going to break the habit of a lifetime for that prat."
Australia coach Ewen McKenzie

"It's some craic! All we wanted to do tonight was play a bit of ball and, f*cking, we did that, and I am f*cking delighted!"
Munster scrum-half Paddy Patterson turns the air blue after defeating South Africa 'A'

Murray Deaker: "Have you ever thought of writing your autobiography?"
New Zealand's Tana Umaga: "On what?"

"The journo was as confused as a goldfish with dementia."
Australia's Nick Cummins

Reporter: "What's your next role after the World Cup?"
Eddie Jones of Japan: "Sit back, enjoy and criticise and be like Clive Woodward and get a job on the television. That's my dream."

"I'd like to thank the press from the heart of my bottom."
Nick Easter after England's win over Australia silenced the press

Reporter: "What went through your head during that scrum?"

Martin Johnson: "Nearly my spine."

After a tough clash against New Zealand

"Pardon my French, but I thought we showed massive balls to go out there and play like that."

Ireland's Andy Farrell

"Why are you shaking your head? I haven't finished answering your question yet. If you want to bet on England losing to France, fine."

Clive Woodward to a French journalist who questioned England's tactics against Wales

"Far be it for me to criticise the referee but I saw him after the match and he was heading straight for the opticians. Guess who he bumped into on the way? Everyone."

Scotland's Ian McLauchlan

Journalist: "What of the future for Welsh rugby?"

Wales captain Mike Watkins: "Over to the Angel for a lot of pints."

Jim Rosenthal: "Do England have a chance of winning the Rugby World Cup?"

Martin Johnson: "Well, we are in the final and nobody else is yet."

FIELD OF DREAMS

"Every time I went to tackle him, Horrocks went one way, Taylor went the other, and all I got was the bloody hyphen."

Nick England on attempts to thwart Phil Horrocks-Taylor

"When he moved away and I saw the blood streaming from the eye, I thought, 'Oh God, I could be in trouble here'."

Martin Johnson on whacking Saracens hooker Robbie Russell

"Don't swear, now, you're on telly, mun."

Nigel Owens to New Zealand's Dan Carter

"I've got a sore neck from looking down one end of the field for the entire second half."

Scotland's Scott Johnson after 6 Nations defeat to England

"Ah, they can't sledge for sh*t! Whitey [Nic White] will be chirpy like always, but the rest of them aren't very witty or smart!"

Ireland's Mack Hansen on the Aussies' sledging

"What we have to do now is tinkle with the little bits."

Scotland lock Scott Murray after defeat to South Africa

"It felt like I had run into a brick sh*t house."

South Africa's Thinus Delport on being tackled by New Zealand's Jerry Collins

"It's like kissing your sister."

Springboks coach Heyneke Meyer on playing the World Cup third-place game

"Maybe he was keen to get to the bathroom, who knows?"

World Rugby's Brett Gosper on why referee Craig Joubert sprinted off the field after a Scotland v Australia clash

"Sort of desolate, decayed, the smell of – I don't want to dramatise it – but death, you know. That is what it feels like, no-man's land, and it is not a nice place to be."
New Zealand's Anton Oliver gets slightly dramatic about the team's dressing room mood after defeat to France

"A player of ours has been proven guilty of biting. That's a scar that will never heal."
Bath coach Andy Robinson after his prop Kevin Yates took a chunk out of an opposing flanker's ear

"I could hardly kiss him, could I? We did realise we were hugging each other for a little bit too long, though – and moved on to find someone else to do it to!"

Will Greenwood embraced Jonny Wilkinson at the end of the 2003 World Cup final

"I'm straighter than that one."

Nigel Owens, who is openly gay, to a hooker during a wonky Harlequins line-out

"We actually got the winning try three minutes from the end, but then they scored."

Australia's Phil Waugh

"Get off, you look ugly."

Aussie referee to England's Neil Back after he grumbled about being ordered to the blood bin against South Africa

"It was not possible for my players to turn the other cheek, as that was being punched as well."

Pontypridd manager Eddie Jones on a bar room brawl after their match with CA Brive

"Two sausages at tonight's barbecue, please."

Phil Kearns claims it's what he said to New Zealand's Sean Fitzpatrick while making a two-fingered gesture to him after scoring

"For an 18-month suspension, I feel I probably should have torn it off. Then at least I could say, 'Look, I've returned to South Africa with the guy's ear'."

South Africa's Johan le Roux on chomping the ear of New Zealand's Sean Fitzpatrick

"There was one particularly uncomfortable scrum on nine minutes when we got lifted off the floor. If I was their scrum coach watching that I would have retired to Panama by now with a cigar."

Lions coach Graham Rowntree on South Africa's scrummage

"In one match last year, eight water-bottle runners ran on the field and gave drinks to the players when someone was injured in the first 30 seconds of the game. Thirty seconds – hell they must have been thirsty. When I played we got a piece of orange at half-time, and if you were quick, you got two."

Colin Meads of New Zealand

"A big man goes down from a slap in the face. I'd be more embarrassed about that. It's wrong because I've seen worse cuddles."

Worcester Warriors coach Dean Ryan on Northampton's Sam Dickinson

PUNDIT PARADISE

"Everyone knows that I have been pumping Martin Leslie for a couple of seasons now."

New Zealand broadcaster Murray Mexted

"Watching France at the moment is like watching clowns at the circus."

Jeremy Guscott

"Australia must feel like they've revisited the scene of an accident, and crashed again."

A TV commentator talking to Michael Lynagh after the quarter-final defeat by England

"Seat of the edge stuff."

Matt Dawson describes the tension in the France-England match

Commentator: "The Frenchman took a bit of a shoeing there, didn't he Brian?"

Brian Moore: "I don't care, he's a Frenchman."

"The All Blacks second-rowers are huge men. They're both over one metre tall… hang on, that would make them midgets."

Murray Mexted

"[Mike] Rafter again doing much of the unseen work which the crowd relishes so much."

Bill McLaren

"The ref's turned a blind ear."

Murray Mexted

"And Dusty Hare kicked 19 of the 17 points."

David Coleman

"Andrew Mehrtens loves it when Daryl Gibson comes inside of him."

New Zealand commentator

"Scotland were victims of their own failure."

Gavin Hastings

"You don't like to see hookers going down on players like that."

Murray Mexted

"Just watch the pace of the French defence. They are attacking the Irish defensively."

Aussie commentator David Fordham

"That kick was absolutely unique, except for the one before it which was identical."

Tony Brown

"They can be almost Fijian in the way they show Gallic flair."

Josh Lewsey on France

"He's looking for some meaningful penetration into the back-line."

Murray Mexted

"They've got their heads in the sand. It's a Canute job."

Anonymous commentator

"There's no doubt about it, he's a big b*stard."

Gavin Hastings on Jonah Lomu

"The ball is often a handicap in these conditions."

Nigel Starmer-Smith

"What a great-sounding name. He sounds like a drug dealer from Brazil."

Murray Mexted on All Black Rico Gear

"And the blue and white hoops of Sale will no doubt act as a red flag to the Tigers."

Commentator Ian Brown

"A lot of these guys have waited a lifetime not to win this."

David Campese

"I think rugby is self-regulating, you don't really need a referee. If someone belts me I'll belt them back, sort of thing."

Jason Leonard

"Strangely, in slow-motion replay, the ball seemed to hang in the air for even longer."

Murray Mexted

"It was blood-curdling stuff, and English blood was curdled to the point where it all drained into their boots."

Martin Johnson

"And there's Gregor Townsend's knee, looking very disappointed."

Gavin Hastings

Producer: "Murray, can you hear me? Murray, can you hear me?

Murray Mexted: "No."

Testing the sound before a South Africa fixture

"I've never seen thighs that big before."

Kenny Logan remarks on Fiji's Rupeni Caucaunibuca

"I don't like this new law, because your first instinct when you see a man on the ground is to go down on him."

Murray Mexted

"What's going on?! Amazing! Mitterand, Platini – your boys took a hell of a beating!"

Will Greenwood after England's semi-final victory over France

"Mothers keep their photo on the mantelpiece to stop the kids going too near the fire."

Broadcaster Jim Noilly on the Munster pack

"Michalik goes for the drop goal... and it's a wibbly wobbly one."

Miles Harrison

"Andy Ellis – the 21-year-old, who turned 22 a few weeks ago."

Murray Mexted

"Nigel Starmer-Smith had seven craps for England some seven years ago."

Jimmy Hill

"Props are crafty as a bag of weasels."

Bill McLaren

"Craig Joubert you are a disgrace and should never referee again! How dare you sprint off the pitch after that decision!"

Matt Dawson on a late penalty decision against Scotland

"There's nothing that a tight forward likes more than a loosie right up his backside."

Murray Mexted

"When they ran onto the field it was like watching a tribe of white orcs on steroids."

Michael Laws on the 2003 England pack

"Well either side could win it, or it could be a draw."

Murray Mexted

"Hopefully the rain will hold off for both sides."

Lawrence Dallaglio

"And in contrast, we have the New Zealand team littered with internationals."

BBC commentator

"The convicts will smash the toffs."

David Campese

"He scored that try after only 22 seconds –
totally against the run of play."

Murray Mexted

"An easy kick for George Fairbairn now but, as
everybody knows, no kicks are easy."

David Doyle-Davidson

"I don't know where Jonny Wilkinson is. I do
know where he is, he's not there."

Brian Moore

"Spread out in a bunch."

Noel Murphy

"If I've seen two more competitive players than Armstrong and Van der Westhuizen, I've yet to see them."

Gavin Hastings

"I would not say he [Rico Gear] is the best left winger in the Super 14, but there are none better."

Murray Mexted

"I look at Colin Meads and see a great big sheep farmer who carried the ball in his hands as though it was an orange pip."

Bill McLaren

"They trained like Tarzan all week and then played like Jane."

Wayne Smith

"I just love it when Mehrtens comes on the inside of Marshall."

Murray Mexted

"Don't touch it, you half-wit."

Brian Moore

"He seized this game by the scruff of his teeth."

James Burridge

"That guy is so quick, he can switch off the light and get into bed before the room is dark."

Jack Gibson

"And there's [Bill] Beaumont in that English scrum looking like a man who enjoys his food."

Bill McLaren

"It's 50-50... in Wales' favour."

Ian Robertson

"And George Gregan is being molested at the breakdown."

ITV commentator

"We want consistency, but we don't want a consistent referee to consistently blow the whistle."

Murray Mexted

"England aren't the same team as four years ago, they haven't got big Johnsons."

Ireland's Newstalk Radio presenter on England's World Cup chances

"Andy Powell goes into the tackle there and he's just not strong enough, he's stripped like a baby."

Stuart Barnes on the Lions v Southern Kings game

"If there's one sight more frightening that the Argentinian front row, it's the Argentinian front row singing."

Welsh TV commentator after the anthems of the opening match in the Rugby World Cup

"Apologies about the colour clash out there. If you're confused, the All Blacks tend to be the team with the ball."

World Cup TV coverage of New Zealand v Scotland

"Olly Barkley puts out. And he puts out well!"

ITV Commentator

Also available